OCT 2000

D1309266

WOMEN'S PRO BASKETBALL TODAY

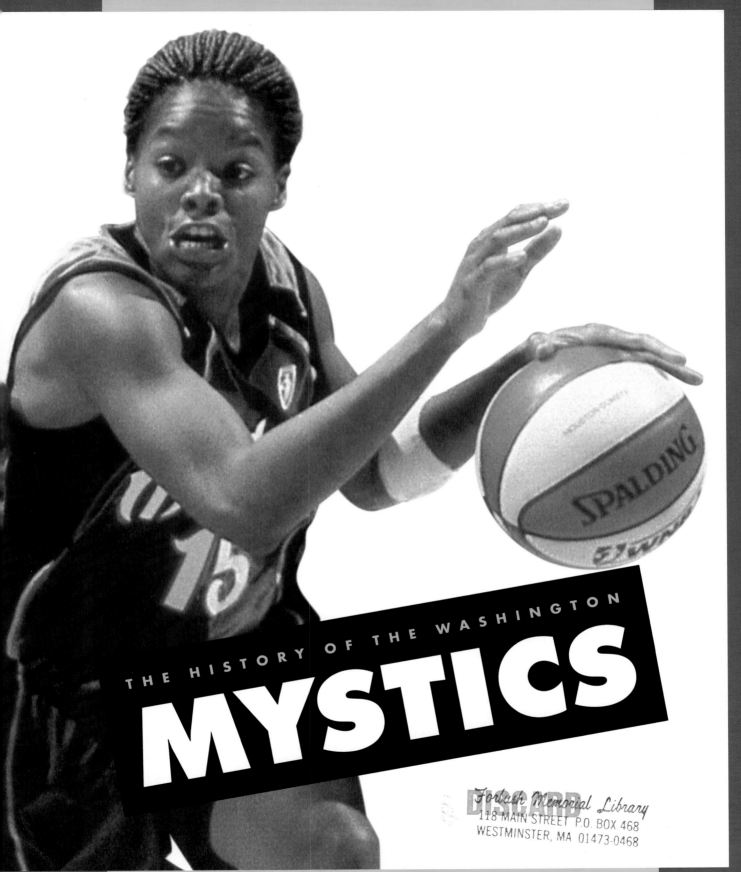

THE HISTORY OF THE WASHINGTON

MYSTICS

DISCARD

Forbush Memorial Library
118 MAIN STREET P.O. BOX 468
WESTMINSTER, MA 01473-0468

REBECCA DAVIS

Published by Creative Education
123 South Broad Street, Mankato, Minnesota 56001
Creative Education is an imprint of The Creative Company

Design by Stephanie Blumenthal
Cover design by Kathy Petelinsek
Production design by Andy Rustad

Photos by: NBA Photos

Copyright © 2000 Creative Education.
International copyrights reserved in all countries.
No part of this book may be reproduced in any form
without written permission from the publisher.
Printed in the United States of America.

Library of Congress Cataloging-in-Publication Data

Davis, Rebecca, 1956-
The History of the Washington Mystics / by Rebecca Davis.
p. cm. — (Women's pro basketball today)
Summary: Describes the history of the Washington Mystics professional women's
basketball team and profiles some of their leading players.
ISBN: 1-58341-012-0

1. Washington Mystics (Basketball team)—Juvenile literature. 2. Basketball for women—
United States Juvenile literature. [1. Washington Mystics (Basketball team) 2. Women basketball players
3. Basketball players.] I. Title. II. Series: Women's Pro Basketball (Mankato, Minn.)

GV885.52.W39D38 1999   99-18887
796.323'64'09753—dc21   CIP

First Edition

2 4 6 8 9 7 5 3 1

In 1998, the Washington Mystics were a team of mystery. The franchise blew the top off of WNBA attendance records despite posting the worst win-loss record of any team in the league's short history. As the Mystics struggled through their 30-game schedule, winning just three games and losing the rest by mostly large margins, fans packed the MCI Center in Washington, D.C., game after game. Washington's team was the youngest in the league, yet it played with heart every night. Although their youthfulness cost the Mystics many games in their first season, it should also make them one of the league's most dangerous teams in the years ahead. With such dynamic stars as Nikki McCray, Murriel Page, and Rita Williams running the floor in the nation's capital city, Washington fans may soon be cheering for a contender.

MURRIEL PAGE BROUGHT HER PHYSICAL STYLE OF PLAY TO THE MYSTICS.

6-FOOT-3 CENTER

LA'SHAWN BROWN (ABOVE);

GUARD ADRIENNE

SHULER (BELOW)

WOMEN'S HOOPS IN THE NATION'S CAPITAL

It seems only fitting that the United States' capital should support a professional women's basketball team. Since its origins, women's basketball has come a long way. After the game was first introduced to women in 1892, it gradually evolved through the 20th century in the form of unusual formats and regulations: six-player teams, restrictions that allowed only certain players to cross mid-court, and games that used just half of the floor. History took a big step forward in 1997, when women's basketball finally came into its own with the establishment of the Women's National Basketball Association.

As soon as the curtains came down on the league's successful first season with the Houston Comets' triumphant league title in August, WNBA officials began pursuing the idea of bringing two expansion teams into the league in 1998. On October 1, 1997, league president Val Ackerman announced that Washington, D.C., and Detroit, Michigan, were the front-running cities in the WNBA's quest to establish new franchises.

Washington, D.C., was primed for a professional women's sports franchise for many reasons. First, as the capital city of the U.S., it is home to a large number of well-educated and professional women—many of whom hold government-related

DEFENSIVE SPECIALIST RITA WILLIAMS

EXPANSION DRAFT PICKS

HEIDI BURGE (ABOVE)

AND PENNY MOORE (BELOW)

positions. It seemed only natural that a city with such opportunities for women also support professional female athletes.

Washington, D.C., has also been a hotbed for women's basketball at the collegiate level for years. Basketball programs at such schools as George Mason, American, George Washington, Maryland, and Virginia have all given fans a glimpse of top-notch women athletes in action. The area gives tremendous support to the girls' game at the high-school level as well. Summer basketball clinics for young female players in the D.C. area are regularly sold out. All of these factors helped build a foundation of interest and support for the city's prospective team before it was even made official that the MCI Center would be home to a franchise.

Abe Pollin, owner of the Washington Mystics and the National Basketball Association's Washington Wizards, was optimistic from the start that the team would be a hit in the east-coast metropolis. "This is the most important city in the country," he said confidently, "and the most important city in the world will support the WNBA. We will be very successful."

Rebecca Lobo, a star center with the New York Liberty and one of the WNBA's most well-known personalities, agreed that Washington would be a step in the right direction for both the city and the league. "[It's] important to have franchises in all the big cities like D.C.," she explained. "[T]he fact that this is our nation's capital makes it that much more important to have a team here. This is a wonderful city to play basketball in, and it's going to be incredible to play in the MCI Center.

Everything's been done so first-class for this league that it makes sense to add another first-class organization."

Washington fans ordered almost 6,000 season-ticket packages in the first two months tickets were on sale. After seeing the level of support present among Washington's fans, the WNBA officially announced on November 11, 1997, that the city would receive an expansion team, with the other franchise being awarded to Detroit, Michigan. On December 16, Abe Pollin announced the name of the new WNBA team: the Washington Mystics. It had been more than a century in coming, but after one exciting and ground-breaking WNBA season, a franchise had landed in the nation's capital.

NIKKI MCCRAY JOINS THE WNBA FRAY

Jim Lewis was named head coach of the Mystics on December 29, 1997. The thrilled coach left his 14-year position as head women's coach at George Mason in the middle of the college season to accept the offer. Lewis came to Washington on the heels of a 201–177 tenure at George Mason. He had also spent time on the coaching staffs of several U.S. women's national teams.

Washington cemented its franchise cornerstone on January 27, 1998, when the WNBA assigned guard Nikki McCray to the roster. McCray spent 1997 playing in the American Basketball

GUARD DEBORAH

CARTER (ABOVE);

THE MYSTICS WERE 2-16

UNDER JIM LEWIS (LEFT).

ALESSANDRA SANTOS DE OLIVEIRA

League, a rival women's professional organization. The 5-foot-11 guard dominated the league, leading her team—the Columbus Quest—to the league championship and earning the Most Valuable Player award. The 25-year-old was widely known as a young star who was equally skilled at both ends of the floor.

After watching the excitement and high-profile exposure of the WNBA from afar in 1997, McCray decided to join the thriving young league. By coming into the league in '98, McCray knew that she would be drafted by either the Detroit Shock or the Washington Mystics. League president Val Ackerman, like many WNBA executives, was delighted with McCray's arrival. "She's a versatile player and a proven scorer who makes things happen on the court," Ackerman explained. "She also has a dynamic personality, and we are certain that she will connect with WNBA fans around the world."

But McCray's basketball success ran much deeper than her professional experience. During her four-year college career at Tennessee, she led the Lady Vols to a combined 122–11 record and four conference titles. After graduating in 1995, she played on the 1996 women's Olympic team, which captured gold in Atlanta, Georgia. Her college coach, Pat Summitt, knew that McCray had the talent and work ethic to go far as a professional. "Nikki continually pays the price, unlike a lot of players I've worked with and watched," she said. "Most athletes with Nikki's talents simply don't put in the time. . . . She's already a great player, but she'll get even better."

WASHINGTON FANS SET SIX ATTENDANCE RECORDS IN 1998 (ABOVE); KERI CHACONAS (BELOW)

NAME: Nikki McCray

BORN: December 17, 1972 (Collierville, Tenn.)

POSITION: Guard

HEIGHT: 5-foot-11

COLLEGE: Tennessee '95

McCray, the former ABL MVP, entered the WNBA in 1998 and finished fourth in league scoring average and sixth in minutes per game. She led her teammates in scoring, assists, and minutes, missing only one start in 30 games. On June 13th she scored a game-high 26 points in a loss to Utah, but six nights later in a rematch she helped Washington to a win with a career-best 29 points and six assists.

STATISTICS: 512 career points

Year	Average	Total Points	Avg. Assists
1998	17.7	512	3.1

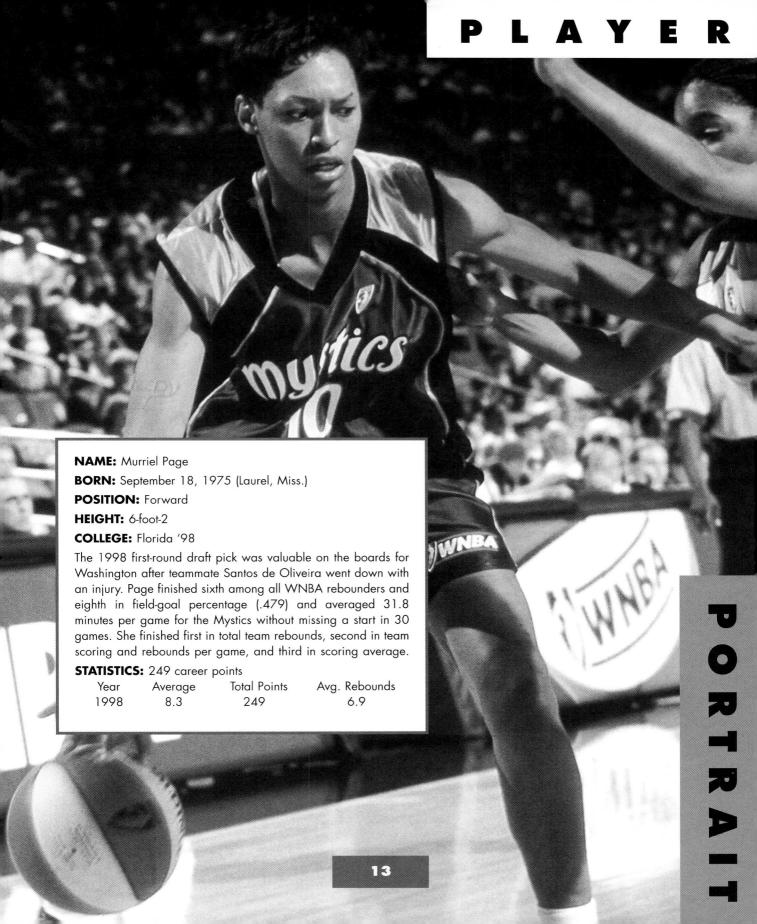

NAME: Murriel Page

BORN: September 18, 1975 (Laurel, Miss.)

POSITION: Forward

HEIGHT: 6-foot-2

COLLEGE: Florida '98

The 1998 first-round draft pick was valuable on the boards for Washington after teammate Santos de Oliveira went down with an injury. Page finished sixth among all WNBA rebounders and eighth in field-goal percentage (.479) and averaged 31.8 minutes per game for the Mystics without missing a start in 30 games. She finished first in total team rebounds, second in team scoring and rebounds per game, and third in scoring average.

STATISTICS: 249 career points

Year	Average	Total Points	Avg. Rebounds
1998	8.3	249	6.9

DEBORAH CARTER (ABOVE);

BRAZILIAN CENTER

ALESSANDRA SANTOS DE

OLIVEIRA (BELOW)

Prior to her professional career, McCray's biggest impact may have been as a defensive player during international competition in 1993. That year, during the COPABA Women's World Championship Qualifying Tournament in Brazil, Brazilian star Hortencia de Fatima shredded the United States team with 37 points in a preliminary-round win. In the tournament finals, the U.S. team again squared off against the Brazilians; this time, the 21-year-old McCray guarded Hortencia de Fatima. Brazil's star netted just two of her 15 points while McCray was guarding her, and the U.S. team captured gold medals.

When she turned professional and donned the uniform of the Columbus Quest, McCray's offensive game took off too. She trampled defenses with nearly 20 points per game and connected on 36 percent of her shots from behind the three-point arc.

By January 27, 1998, when she signed with the WNBA and was assigned to the Mystics, 24-year-old Alessandra Santos de Oliveira had already competed professionally for six seasons. The 6-foot-5 Brazilian also had a wealth of international experience that included the America's Cup championship, the World Cup championship, and a medal-winning performance at the 1996

PLAYOFF VETERAN PENNY MOORE

Olympic Games in Atlanta. Mystics coaches and officials saw the tall young center—known for her relentless rebounding—as a fine complement to the high-scoring McCray.

HOOP DREAMS IN D.C.

In the league's expansion draft on February 18, 1998, the Mystics added former Los Angeles Sparks forward Heidi Burge to their roster. The 6-foot-5 Burge—who is in the Guinness Book of World Records with her sister Heather as the tallest female identical twins in the world—was a four-year starter at Virginia. Her fierce rebounding helped lead the Cavaliers to three Atlantic Coast Conference championships.

Guard Penny Moore was the Mystics' second pick in the expansion draft. Moore played in all 28 games in 1997 for the Charlotte Sting and was outstanding in the Sting's semifinals play-off game against the Houston Comets. Standing six feet tall and blessed with great leaping ability, she can play either the forward or guard position. Before joining the WNBA in '97, Moore played professionally in Italy, Luxembourg, and Finland, where she consistently averaged double digits in both points and rebounds per game. Washington team officials drafted the athletic 29-year-old to provide both leadership and point-production.

Powerful 6-foot guard Deborah Carter, Washington's third pick in the expansion draft, came to Washington,

ADRIENNE SHULER (ABOVE); HEIDI BURGE AVERAGED 6.7 POINTS PER GAME IN 1998 (RIGHT).

D.C., from the Utah Starzz. The Mystics then filled out their roster with other impressive young players in the WNBA's April 29th draft, including 6-foot-2 forward Murriel Page, one of the best players in the history of Florida Gators' basketball. "La," (Murriel's nickname and real first name) claims that she picked up her physical style of play by playing dirt-court basketball with uncles and male cousins who would rather knock her down than have her make a shot over them.

Rita Williams, a feisty 5-foot-6 guard who specializes in defensive play, was the Mystics' second-round pick. Williams came to Washington straight from the University of Connecticut, where she had helped her team to a combined 93–8 record during her career and earned All-American honors. Coach Jim Lewis also added one of his former players—George Mason basketball standout and sharpshooter Keri Chaconas—to the team.

The final roster was exceedingly young—with an average age of 25 and no player older than 29—but the combination of raw ability and variety of experience created a potentially strong and exciting lineup.

FEISTY RITA WILLIAMS (ABOVE); FORMER UTAH GUARD DEBORAH CARTER (BELOW)

KERI CHACONAS AVERAGED

4.8 POINTS (ABOVE);

ADRIENNE SHULER

(BELOW)

TRIALS AND TRIUMPHS

After a short training camp, the Mystics opened their season against the Sting in Charlotte, North Carolina. McCray led Washington's attack with 19 points, and Deborah Carter and Penny Moore each pulled down five rebounds. Despite the strong efforts of the young trio, the Mystics were outgunned by the veteran Sting and fell to defeat 83–57.

The next game was a heartbreaker in Utah against the Starzz. Big center Alessandra Santos de Oliveira posted the Mystics' first double-double, pulling down an incredible 18 boards and scoring 19 points. McCray netted 26 points, and Deborah Carter was a thorn in the Starzz's side from all angles, recording eight points, three rebounds, three assists, and three steals. Still, the Mystics would have to wait for their first win, as the Starzz squeaked out a 78–77 victory.

The Mystics played their third straight road game—and suffered their third straight loss—at Phoenix before returning to Washington for their home opener against Utah. The momentous occasion in the MCI Center would be a sign of things to come, as thousands of enthusiastic fans packed the stands. That night, the

women of D.C. showed the heart and potential that would endear them to fans. The Mystics' offense and defense were both stunning, and the team flew out to a 29–12 lead midway through the first half. Washington's shooters were red-hot, hitting 12 of their first 20 shots, and their rigid defense forced the Starzz into eight turnovers in the game's first 10 minutes.

By halftime, Washington's lead had shrunk to 44–36, but it was by far the Mystics' best half of the young season. McCray had connected on three of four three-point attempts and went into the locker room with 14 points. Rita Williams, meanwhile, had dismantled the Starzz with four assists and three steals in the game's first 20 minutes.

The Mystics continued to play at a high level in the second half, but Utah hung around, keeping the score close. Then the Mystics fell into a three-minute scoring drought, and the Starzz crept even closer. But in the last two minutes, McCray took charge, hitting two crucial turnaround jumpers to break Utah's run and preserve an 85–76 win. McCray ended up with a season-high 29 points, and Alessandra Santos de Oliveira posted 14 points and pulled down seven boards. Murriel Page, Rita Williams, and Penny Moore each finished with 11 points as well. The joyous crowd went crazy, and McCray, whose face had been a constant expression of determination throughout the game, finally flashed her trademark smile as she ran around the court with her arms raised triumphantly.

FORMER HEAD COACH JIM LEWIS (ABOVE); MURRIEL PAGE (BELOW)

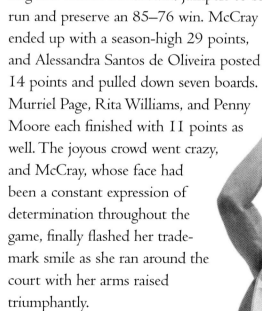

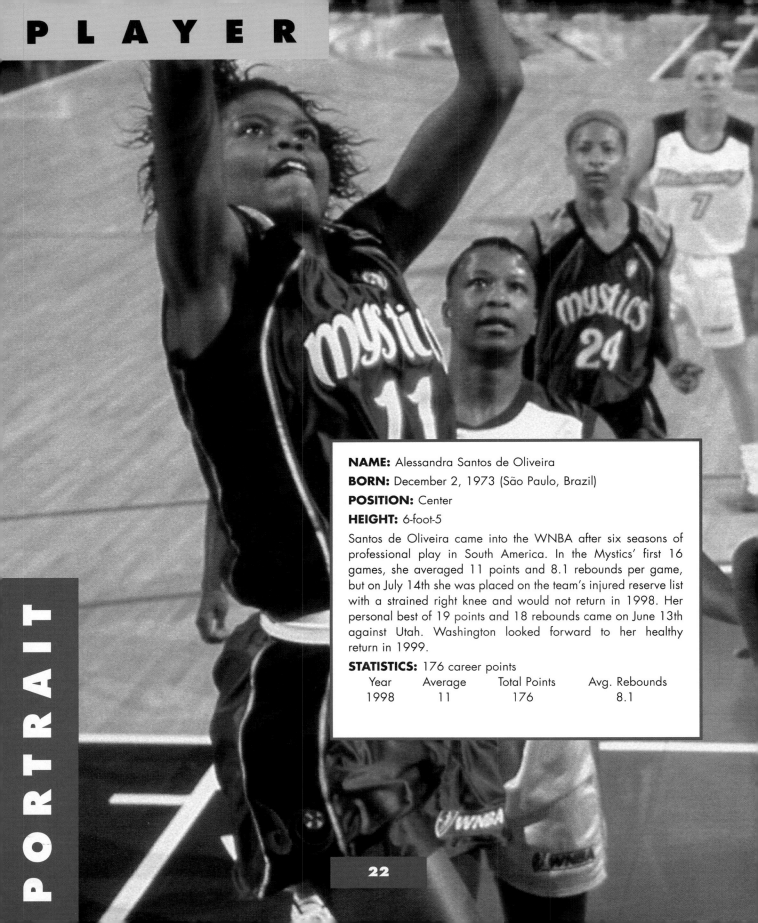

NAME: Alessandra Santos de Oliveira

BORN: December 2, 1973 (São Paulo, Brazil)

POSITION: Center

HEIGHT: 6-foot-5

Santos de Oliveira came into the WNBA after six seasons of professional play in South America. In the Mystics' first 16 games, she averaged 11 points and 8.1 rebounds per game, but on July 14th she was placed on the team's injured reserve list with a strained right knee and would not return in 1998. Her personal best of 19 points and 18 rebounds came on June 13th against Utah. Washington looked forward to her healthy return in 1999.

STATISTICS: 176 career points

Year	Average	Total Points	Avg. Rebounds
1998	11	176	8.1

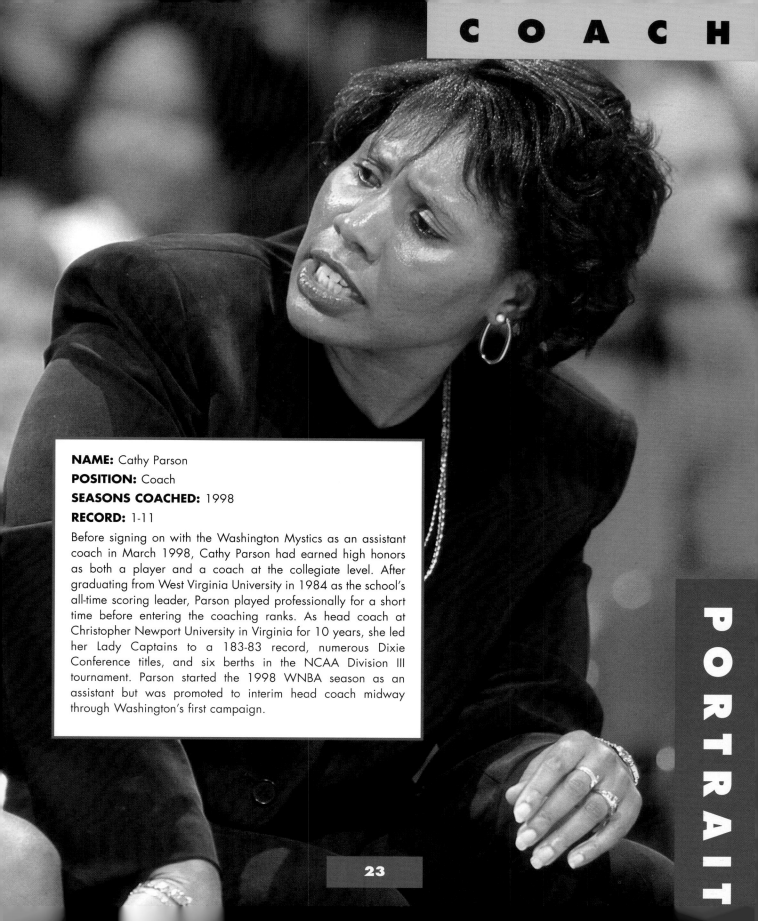

NAME: Cathy Parson

POSITION: Coach

SEASONS COACHED: 1998

RECORD: 1-11

Before signing on with the Washington Mystics as an assistant coach in March 1998, Cathy Parson had earned high honors as both a player and a coach at the collegiate level. After graduating from West Virginia University in 1984 as the school's all-time scoring leader, Parson played professionally for a short time before entering the coaching ranks. As head coach at Christopher Newport University in Virginia for 10 years, she led her Lady Captains to a 183-83 record, numerous Dixie Conference titles, and six berths in the NCAA Division III tournament. Parson started the 1998 WNBA season as an assistant but was promoted to interim head coach midway through Washington's first campaign.

PORTRAIT

DURABLE GUARD

PENNY MOORE STARTED

26 GAMES IN 1998.

LEARNING THE HARD WAY

After their victory at the MCI Center, the Mystics slid into an eight-game losing streak. Some games were close, but many others weren't. Still, the fans packed the MCI Center, supporting their team with an extraordinary loyalty. The players would respond to the support with some strong individual performances throughout the summer season. Penny Moore applied heavy defensive pressure all over the court, forward Heidi Burge shot a team-high .509 from the floor, and guard Keri Chaconas blazed away from long-distance, hitting 30 three-pointers for the year.

All three wins in 1998 were on the Mystics' home court, with the last two coming on July 11 against their sister expansion team, the Detroit Shock, and on August 9 against the Los Angeles Sparks. McCray continued to shine, scoring 21 points in each win. Alessandra Santos de Oliveira also continued to lead Washington in rebounding; against the physical Detroit team, she pulled down 14 boards. Unfortunately, that brilliant performance would be one of her last in 1998, as she went down with a season-ending knee injury shortly afterward.

In Houston, facing the powerful league champions two days after their victory over Detroit, the Mystics held their own, staying within seven points of the defending champs for 30 minutes. But the Comets then started hammering Washington, stringing consecutive baskets together until the game was out of reach. When the final horn sounded, the score stood at 81–67.

To few fans' surprise, coach Jim Lewis was fired 18 games into the season. Washington's record at that point was 2–16—the worst in the league— and Mystics officials felt that the team had enough talent to be much higher in the standings. Cathy Parson, the team's assistant coach, was named interim head coach.

THE MYSTICS WENT
1-11 UNDER CATHY
PARSON (ABOVE);
HEIDI BURGE (BELOW)

KERI CHACONAS

(ABOVE); LA'SHAWN

BROWN (BELOW)

Parson had graduated from West Virginia University and played in the short-lived Women's American Basketball Association before moving into the coaching ranks. As head coach at Providence College for three seasons, she led her squad to a Big East Conference championship and a berth in the women's NIT tournament. She then moved on to become head coach at Christopher Newport University, where she led the Lady Captains to eight Dixie Conference regular-season titles, three conference tournament crowns, and six NCAA Division III tournament berths.

Although the players were happy with the change, wins did not come any easier down the season's final stretch. The young team from the east coast still lost 11 of its final 12 games.

The Mystics' final win came over Los Angeles on August 9. Six days earlier in another matchup with the Sparks, Penny Moore had burned L.A. for a career-high 18 points, but the Mystics still lost by 14. When the Sparks came to Washington, the Mystics had revenge on their minds. Forward Murriel Page led the low-post attack by scoring 12 points and pulling down eight rebounds, while Nikki McCray piled up 21 points and handed out four assists.

The hero of the game, however, was guard Adrienne Shuler, who sank a game-winning 12-foot bank shot with 3.8 seconds left on the clock. Shuler finished the game with 14 total

points—including three field goals from three-point range—five rebounds, and five assists. Although the win was a rarity in the Mystics' dismal first season, it was an encouraging sign of the young team's balanced offensive potential.

A SEASON FOR THE BOOKS

The Washington Mystics' first year was one of the strangest seasons in recent professional sports history. It was both a terrible disaster and a brilliant triumph. When the *Washington Post* asked Mystics team officials if 1998 had been a successful first year, general manager Wes Unseld said no. Mystics president Susan O'Malley disagreed, calling the season "a huge success. We couldn't have asked for more." O'Malley was referring to the incredible fan support; Unseld was looking at the team's win-loss record.

Fans in the MCI Center were almost a sixth player on the floor for the Mystics in 1998. A sell-out crowd of 20,674 packed the arena on two occasions, and an average of 15,989 fans per game—50 percent more than the league average—filled the seats over the course of the season. Of the WNBA's top 10 attendance records in 1998, the Mystics set six of them. "I'm as amazed as anybody," Unseld said. "We thought [attendance] was going to be

DEBORAH CARTER (ABOVE);

MYSTICS FANS FILLED

THE MCI CENTER

IN 1998 (BELOW).

okay, but nobody had any idea it was going to play out like it did. . . . The fans just fell in love."

In the Mystics' 27 losses, they were beaten by an average of 15 points, but they always played with courage, never quitting or losing their composure. Nikki McCray believes that this show of spirit is what kept the fans coming back. "I think the difference is the way we relate to the fans. . .," she said. "[T]hat's what makes it worthwhile to come out to do this every night when you're having a difficult season." Others saw the support as recognition of the growing athletic opportunities for women. "I think our start was about girl power," O'Malley said.

Mystics officials know, however, that their team is going to have to produce more wins down the road to fuel the tremendous energy poured forth by Mystics fans. To do that, the team will look to add more talented young players and perhaps a veteran rebounder and shot-blocker to the roster through upcoming drafts and free-agent signings.

KERI CHACONAS (ABOVE);

STAR REBOUNDER

ALESSANDRA SANTOS

DE OLIVEIRA (RIGHT)

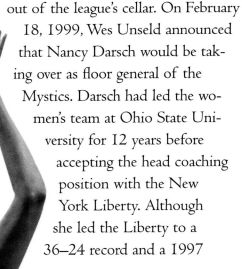

After the 1998 season finale, the Mystics began looking for a new head coach to lead the franchise out of the league's cellar. On February 18, 1999, Wes Unseld announced that Nancy Darsch would be taking over as floor general of the Mystics. Darsch had led the women's team at Ohio State University for 12 years before accepting the head coaching position with the New York Liberty. Although she led the Liberty to a 36–24 record and a 1997

FORMER ABL MVP NIKKI MCCRAY

COACH NANCY DARSCH

HOPES TO TURN

WASHINGTON'S

FORTUNES AROUND.

playoff victory in her two seasons in New York, Liberty officials opted not to renew her contract.

Unseld saw New York's loss as Washington's gain. "Nancy Darsch is a tremendously talented coach, and we are excited to make her a part of the Mystics," he said. "She brings a wealth of professional, [NCAA] Division I, and Olympic experience with her. This experience, combined with her winning attitude, will help make the Mystics competitive this summer."

On May 4, 1999, the Mystics continued to brighten their future by selecting 6-foot-2 forward Chamique Holdsclaw with the first pick in the WNBA draft. The two-time National Player of the Year—whose dominance and talent reminded many fans of former NBA star Michael Jordan—had led Tennessee to three straight national titles from 1996 to 1998 and averaged 21.3 points and 8.1 boards per game as a senior. "She's the player of the present and the player of the future for our league," WNBA president Val Ackerman said.

The team's rising young stars—including Holdsclaw, Nikki McCray, Murriel Page, and Rita Williams—have the potential to form one of the league's most dangerous and exciting starting line-ups. McCray established herself as one of the WNBA's hottest stars in 1998, averaging 17.7 points and 1.5 steals per game. After Santos de Oliveira was knocked out of the lineup, Page stepped up to lead the Mystics with nearly seven rebounds a night in addition to her 8.3 points-per-game average. Williams also demonstrated her versatility by stealing the ball a team-best 63 times and handing out 69 assists.

Both Nikki McCray and Murriel Page were selected as members of the U.S. National Team in the 2000 Olympic Games—a sign of good things to come in Washington, D.C. As the saying goes, there is no substitute for youth, and Washington has plenty of it. With their raw talent and unmatched fan support, the Mystics may soon be casting their spell on the WNBA.